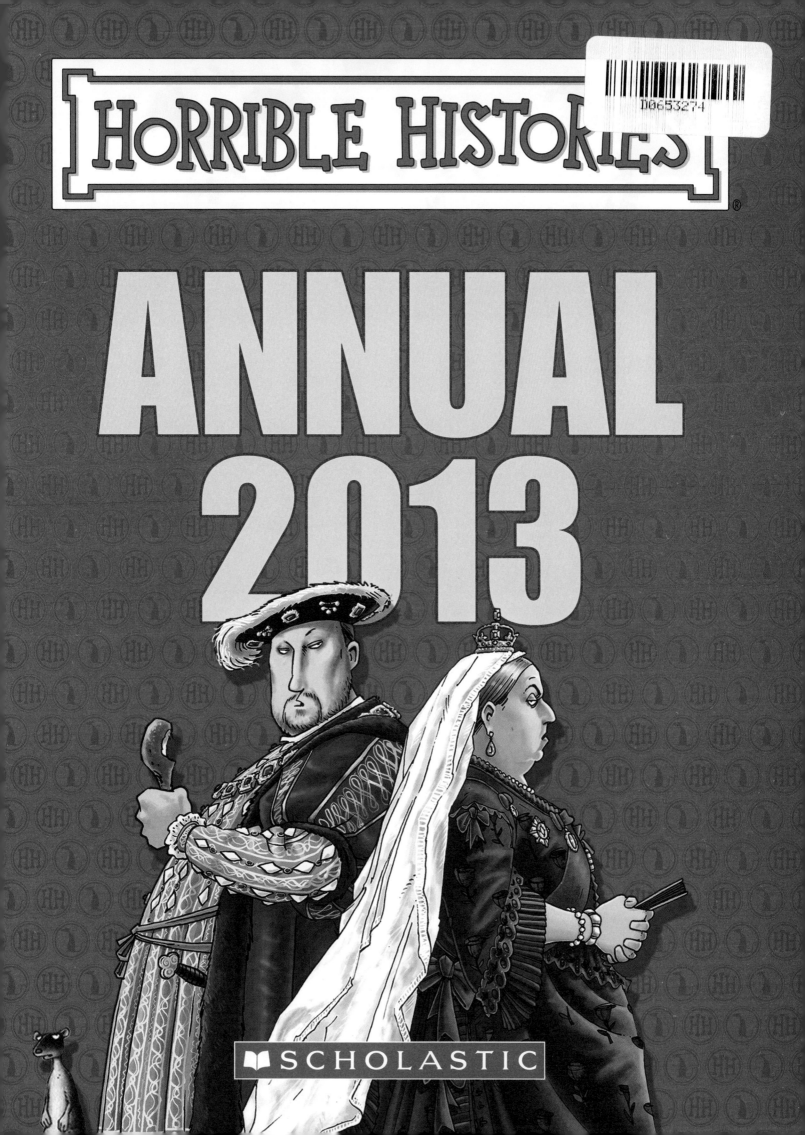

CONTENTS

THERE'S A LOT TO GET YOUR TEETH INTO!

FOUL FACTS ABOUT ME

☠ If I could go back in time, I'd go back to

☠ My knight name would be

☠ If I were King or Queen for a day, my first law would be

☠ The most horrible person in history was

☠ My favourite Horrible Histories book is

☠ If I were a pirate, my ship would be called

☠ If I could invite any three people from history to a party, I'd invite

------------------, -------------- and ----------

WANTED

Draw a picture of yourself here.

NAME: _____

ALIAS: _____

WANTED FOR: _____

MOST HORRIBLE HABIT: _____

REWARD: _____

IT'S CRIMINAL!

Vermin K's HORRIBLE HOT SEAT

Hello and welcome to HORRIBLE HOTSEAT!
Please welcome your host... Mr Vermin K!

Well hello there Horrible Histories fans!
Can you tell which of these 'facts' are terribly true – and which are frightfully false? If you can, take your place in the Horrible Hotseat for a chance to win a priceless gold crown*! Are you sitting uncomfortably? Then I'll begin...

1. There were dentists around in Stone Age times.

2. In London during the Blitz, church bells could only be rung when it was time for everyone to go home.

3. The cut-throat Celts wore armour when they went to war.

4. French soldiers during the First World War were taken to the front line of the Battle of Marne by taxi.

5. The Ancient Greek slave, Aesop, who made up fables such as 'The Tortoise and the Hare', was very popular with Greek priests.

6. In the Middle Ages, wedding guests threw rose petals over the bride.

7. Ancient Egyptian doctors believed they could cure tooth ache by putting a dead mouse in the patient's mouth.

8. Inca men were allowed to marry their sisters.

9. Shakespeare invented the word 'lonely'.

10. Queen Elizabeth I died because of a rotten tooth.

I'M THE HOST AND YOU'LL BE TOAST

So how did you do? Did you beat the hot seat or do you have a burnt behind?
Turn to page 60 to see how you've done, and claim your crown!*
Ta ta for now!

Vermin K xxx

*Actually, it's just a picture of a priceless gold crown. But still!

PUTRID PIRATE BATTLE SHIPS

Challenge your mate to a game of Putrid Pirate Battleships and see who ends up in Davey Jones's Locker first...

HOW TO PLAY

1. Pull out or photocopy the page opposite and give two grids, A and B, and a pencil to each player. You'll mark the position of your own ships on grid A, and track where your enemies ships are on grid B.

2. Mark the position of your ships on grid A. You have five different ships to add, and they're all different sizes – have a look at the Pirate Ship Chart. Make sure your enemy can't see where you've put your ships!

3. Take turns to fire at each other by guessing the coordinates of your enemy's ships. When the other player guesses a square where part of one your ships is, shout 'hit!'. When they guess a square where you don't have a ship, shout 'miss!'

4. Mark a hit on grid B with an 'X' in the square. Mark a miss on grid B with an 'O' in the square.

5. Shout out 'Sunk!' when one of your ships has been completely sunk.

6. The winner is the player to sink all of their enemy's ships first!

SHIP	Cruiser	Battleship	Galleon	Schooner	Life raft
NUMBER OF SQUARES	5	4	3	3	1

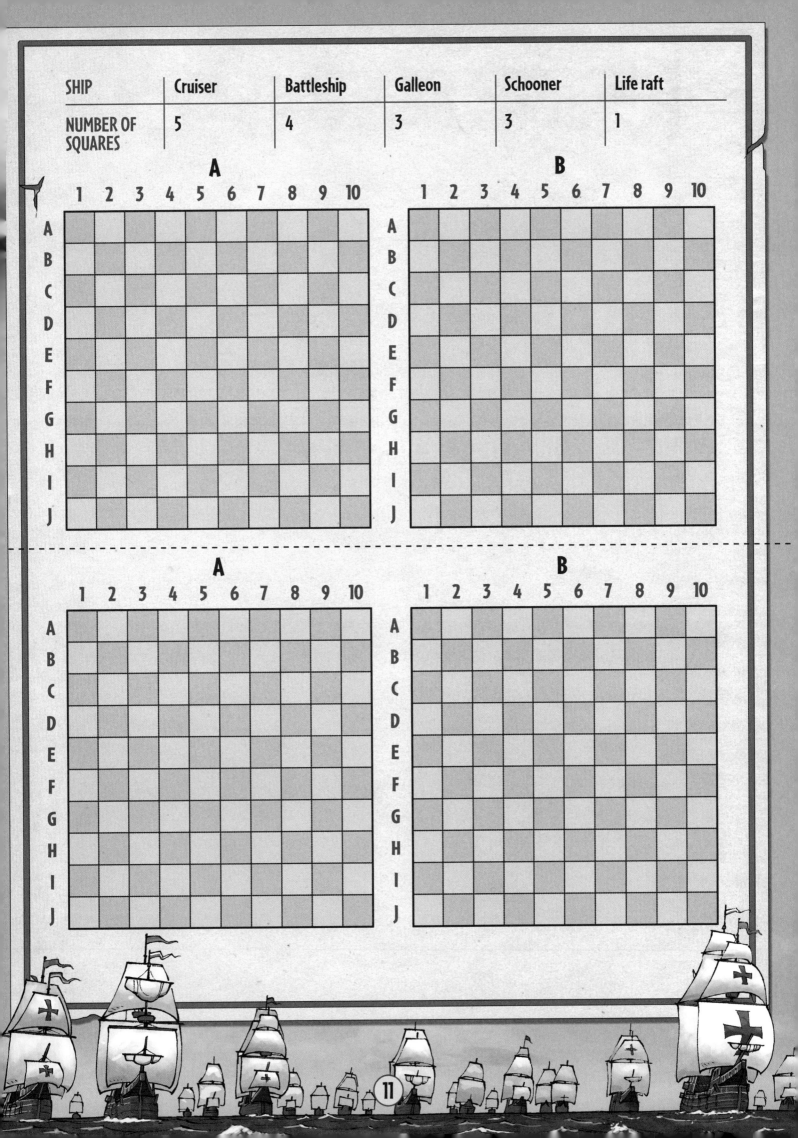

HEARTTHROB KNIGHT IN SHINING ARMOUR

Oi! MAGAZINE

SIR LANCELOT DU LAC

gives an exclusive interview to Oi! Magazine, and shows us around his beautiful home.

Oi: You had quite a difficult childhood, didn't you?

LDL: Well, it started off badly — when I was a baby, I was kidnapped by the Lady of the Lake. That's where I got my weird surname — 'du Lac' means 'of the Lake.' My adopted mum brought me up under water, so I grew up a bit wet.

Oi: But you've turned that around - you're King Arthur's top knight!

LDL: Well I don't like to blow my own trumpet. But yes, yes I am.

Oi: You live in King Arthur's court, Camelot. Can you tell our readers what that's like? It must seem like a castle compared to your childhood home!

LDL: Well, yes. Because it is a castle.

Oi: And you share it with lots of other knights, right?

LDL: Yep - there are 1600 of us. We're like a great big family.

Oi: We've heard you all sit around one table?

LDL: That's right, a ruddy great big round one. It gets a bit cosy at dinner time. By the time someone's passed the salt across the table, your dinner's cold.

Oi: That must be a knight-mare.

LDL: It is, actually. I really hate lukewarm boar's head. But you know me - I never complain.

Oi: Can you tell our readers what a typical day is like for you?

LDL: That's the great thing about being a knight — no two days are the same. Usually I do a little jousting, some feasting, fight a battle or two, rescue a lady from a tower, that sort of thing.

Oi: You're Camelot's most eligible batchelor. Is there a special lady in your life?

LDL: A true knight never tells.

Oi: You've been seen getting rather close to King Arthur's wife Guinevere...

LDL: We're just good friends.

Oi: That's not what we hear —

LDL: No comment. This interview is over.

LONELY HEARTS

WHO'S LOOKING FOR LOVE THIS WEEK?

Sixth time lucky? Cuddly king, unlucky in love, looking for a wife who doesn't look like a horse. Likes: eating, real tennis, having people executed, being in charge. Dislikes: the Pope, wives who answer back, anyone who beats me at wrestling.

Black-toothed beauty, tired of explorers trying to impress her with potatoes, wishes to marry England. England, if you're reading: how about it?

Dear Ratty

The rodent who tells it like it is

Hello readers,
Can you guess which famous people have written to me for advice this week?

Dear Ratty,

I don't know what to do. My beastly brother Ed was supposed to become king after our dad died, but he fell in love with a divorced American. Now he's chucked the crown so he can marry her – and I have to be king! It's not fair! I have a terrible stammer – how am I supposed to give all those speeches?

Yours,
Bewildered of Buckingham Palace

Dear Bewildered,

First of all, you have to be king. If you and your brother both gave up the throne, it would be very embarrassing for your mum. The stammering is a bit of a problem, I agree. Why don't you visit a speech therapist? If all goes well, someone might make a film about you both one day.

Ratty xxx

Dear Ratty,
I'm a bit amazing, me – I'm a brilliant warrior and love nothing more than killing my neighbours and stealing their land. (Don't worry, their dead bodies don't go to waste – I drink out of their skulls, make their bones into flutes, and use their skin as drums. We're big on recycling in Peru.) Anyway – now my snotty little brother has started copying me (as usual). He's conquering people too, and he's getting really powerful. What shall I do?

Yours,
Angry of the Andes

Dear Angry,

I can't believe you're even asking me this question. Have him killed, obviously, and add his skull to your mug collection.

Ratty xxx

13

FOUL FOOD AND ROTTEN RECIPES

Think school dinners are bad? Look at what people ate in the past and stop complaining.

BREAKFAST

WOEFUL SECOND WORLD WAR FADGE

Need to make breakfast on a budget? Have nothing in your cupboard but a few old potatoes and a bit of flour? Then try this Second World War recipe for Fadge! (Warning: 'Fadge' may sound like 'fudge', but it's a lot less tasty. Not recommended for those with tastebuds.)

1. Boil some well-scrubbed potatoes, then peel and mash them while hot.
2. When the mixture is cool enough to handle, add salt and flour, so it becomes a dough.
3. Knead on a well-floured board for about five minutes, then roll into a large circle about 1/2 centimetre thick.
4. Cut into wedge-shaped pieces and cook on a hot griddle or on the upper shelf of an oven until brown on both sides, turning once.
5. Serve - to someone you don't like very much!

LUNCH

AWFUL ANCIENT EGYPTIAN BREAD

The Awful Egyptians ate lots of bread. Unfortunately, it was very gritty – and it wore away their teeth! If you want to know what Ancient Egyptian bread tastes like (without needing a trip to the dentist), try this recipe. For a truly authentic Egyptian lunch, put some raw onion on top.

Ingredients:
4 cups of wholemeal flour
Half a teaspoon of salt
2 cups of warm water

1. Mix the flour, salt and water.
2. Knead well for five minutes.
3. Shape the dough into circles.
4. Place the shapes on a greased baking tray.
5. Leave overnight.
6. Decorate the edges of the shapes by pressing them with your fingers.
7. Bake in an oven at Gas mark 4 for half an hour.

DINNER

ROTTEN ROMAN CHICKEN

The Romans loved throwing banquets and stuffing themselves with things like dormice and snails till they were sick. But sometimes they cooked quite tasty things, like this chicken dish. They didn't make this recipe up – they learned it when they invaded North Africa.

Ingredients:
Chicken pieces (one for each person)
1/4 teaspoon of cumin powder
1/4 teaspoon of coriander seeds
Four dates (chopped into small pieces)
4 tablespoons of chopped nuts
2 tablespoons of honey
2 tablespoons of wine vinegar
1 cube of chicken stock (crumbled in a cup of water)
A pinch of pepper
1 tablespoon of cooking oil
A handful of breadcrumbs

1. Put the chicken pieces in a roasting dish.
2. Brush them with cooking oil, sprinkle them with pepper and cover the dish with cooking foil.
3. Roast the pieces at 350 degrees Farenheit, 180 degrees Celcius or gas mark 4 for 30 minutes.
4. While the chicken is roasting, put the other ingredients into a pan and simmer for 20 minutes to make the Numidian sauce.
5. When the chicken pieces are ready, put them on a serving dish and pour over the sauce.
6. Serve the chicken with vegetables – cabbages and beans are very Roman.

Don't like the sound of those meals? Maybe you'd prefer one of these treats from the Middle Ages. (You'd only have eaten these if you were rich – if you were poor you'd have scraped by with some porridge and a few vegetables.)

Porpoise Pudding – stuffed porpoise stomach

Trojan hog – pig stuffed with birds and shellfish, then roasted

Deer-antler soup – singed antlers, chopped and boiled with wine

Cockentrice – back half of a pig sewn together with front half of a chicken and roasted

Coqz Heaumez – whole roast chicken dressed in helmet and lance, sitting on a roasted hog (as if the hog was a horse)

Mashed deer tongues – served on fried bread

Roast peacock – skinned then roasted, then put back in skin so it looks alive

Pickled puffin – a puffin cooked and soaked in vinegar

Curried head – a warrior's head cooked in curry sauce (that's what Richard I of England ate during the Crusades)

AWFUL EGYPTIANS – SPOT THE LOT

Can you spot all 11?

WOULD YOU RATHER?

Think life was better in the good old days? Think again!

Once you've decided which of these awful alternatives you'd prefer, see if you can guess when in horrible history these things really happened! Turn to page 60 to find out if you're right.

Would you rather...

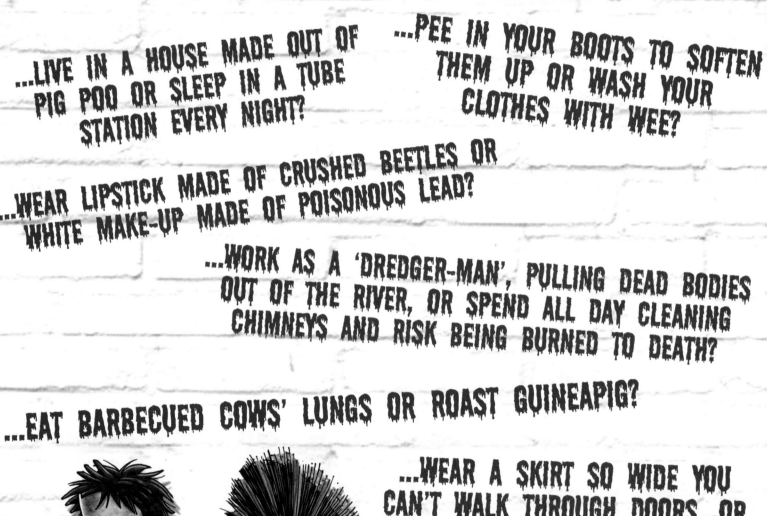

...LIVE IN A HOUSE MADE OUT OF PIG POO OR SLEEP IN A TUBE STATION EVERY NIGHT?

...PEE IN YOUR BOOTS TO SOFTEN THEM UP OR WASH YOUR CLOTHES WITH WEE?

...WEAR LIPSTICK MADE OF CRUSHED BEETLES OR WHITE MAKE-UP MADE OF POISONOUS LEAD?

...WORK AS A 'DREDGER-MAN', PULLING DEAD BODIES OUT OF THE RIVER, OR SPEND ALL DAY CLEANING CHIMNEYS AND RISK BEING BURNED TO DEATH?

...EAT BARBECUED COWS' LUNGS OR ROAST GUINEAPIG?

...WEAR A SKIRT SO WIDE YOU CAN'T WALK THROUGH DOORS, OR AN IRON CORSET SO TIGHT YOU KEEP FAINTING?

IT'S ALL TRUE!

YE OLDE TUDOR WORD SEARCH

P	R	O	T	E	S	T	A	N	T	S	B	N	E	R
R	S	S	K	L	Y	R	N	E	H	J	P	P	X	I
F	H	P	P	L	V	R	P	F	F	O	H	L	N	Q
K	L	T	A	L	M	O	Z	E	P	I	J	I	J	K
F	M	T	O	N	P	I	O	F	O	E	N	C	R	L
L	W	R	L	A	I	D	F	L	H	R	C	E	D	F
E	Q	C	N	M	I	S	F	L	C	K	L	R	D	E
A	B	A	X	E	J	C	H	A	P	L	G	M	P	U
S	C	B	J	K	U	F	N	A	E	R	U	L	H	G
L	X	P	Q	M	E	P	L	Y	R	F	L	B	R	A
Y	U	I	C	R	W	Z	L	V	Z	M	A	M	I	L
T	N	D	O	Q	C	Z	Q	S	R	N	A	O	L	P
I	N	D	P	C	R	Z	B	Y	O	P	E	D	M	F
A	U	P	N	R	R	Y	P	M	D	F	B	N	A	H
T	D	Q	S	M	A	L	L	P	O	X	S	L	O	R

Shakespeare's just finished his new play – but he's missed out some words! Can you help him find them?

TUDOR ✓
PROTESTANTS ✓
SPANISH ARMADA ✓
LICE ✓
SMALL POX ✓
PLAGUE ✓
FLEAS ✓
AXE ✓
CHOP ✓
HENRY ✓

HE'S LOST FOR WORDS?

19

DAFT WAYS TO DIE

ATTILA THE HUN

Attila the Hun was a ruthless warrior who managed to conquer the whole of Asia. He was pretty ruthless when he was looking for a wife, too – he fell in love with Saint Ursula, who didn't fancy marrying him, so he killed her – and 11,000 of her followers. That's what they call over-kill. Daft death: Attila finally convinced someone to marry him, but he got so drunk on his wedding night that he didn't notice he had a nosebleed – and he drowned in his own blood.

RICHARD OF NORMANDY

Richard was one of William the Conqueror's sons. In 1074 Richard was charging through the New Forest on his horse when he collided with a tree. (There were no driving tests for horse riders in those days. If there had been, Richard would have failed.) Richard was carried back to Winchester but his injuries were so bad that he died soon afterwards. William the Conqueror was very upset. (And the tree can't have been too happy, either!)

FREDERICK I

Frederick I was king of Germany and Italy, and he was so religious that the Pope gave him an extra title – Holy Roman Emperor. In 1189, he led a religious war, called a Crusade, to try and conquer the 'Holy Land' in the Middle East, but it seems he didn't have God on his side... One hot day, Thirsty Fred waded into a river to have a drink, but he forgot to take his armour off first. He sank to the bottom of the river and drowned.

FRANZ REICHELT

Franz was a French tailor who was convinced he could design a suit of clothing which would convert into a parachute. On 4 February 1912 he climbed the Eiffel Tower to test his design. Bird-brained Franz thought that if he jumped from the tower wearing the suit, and flapped his arms a bit, he'd fly safely to the ground. Not the best of plans, Franz! The parachute didn't work ... and Franz didn't survive.

HENRY I

Henry I was pretty cunning – he 'accidentally' killed his brother William while they were out hunting so he could be king of England instead of him. But he was also a bit greedy. He really liked eating lampreys – horrible-looking eels with lots of teeth. One day he ate so many of them that he dropped down dead.

IT'S ALL TRUE!

4 PETER SMART'S HOUSE
'I am forced to work at a water mill. Why?'
a) I am an orphan b) my mother sold me to the mill owner c) I am starving

5 ISABELLA READ'S HOUSE
'I am 12 years old. I carry coal underground on my back. How much do I carry at a time?'
a) 57 kilos b) 37 kilos c) 17 kilos

6 SARAH GOODER'S HOUSE
'I am eight years old. I work in the mine and hardly see daylight. What am I frightened of?'
a) the miners b) the pit ponies c) the dark

8 THE PENNILESS PARENT'S HOUSE
'I couldn't afford to feed my new baby. What have I done with it?'
a) sold it b) sold my furniture to buy it food c) dropped it in the canal

7 JAMES MORROW'S HOUSE
'I am eight years old and work in the mine. A coal truck crushed my what?'
a) sandwiches b) leg c) head

17 THE NAIL-MAKER'S HOUSE
'I make sure my boys work hard and punish them if they don't. How do I punish them?'
a) nail their ears to the work bench b) put salt in their tea c) stand on their toes

18 BENJAMIN MILLER'S HOUSE
'I am a pit manager. Why do we use women down the mines?'
a) they're cheap b) they're better workers c) they don't complain as much as men

16 THE FACTORY OVERSEER'S HOUSE
'I often get children to work even longer than 19 hours. How?'
a) I pay them more b) I take the clock out of the factory c) I beat them with a steel rod

20 HERBERT SPENCER'S HOUSE
'I study the workers. I believe...'
a) children should start work at the age of four b) women should not work at all c) weak workers dying is good for the country

The End

19 THE FACTORY DOCTOR'S HOUSE
'I have noticed that the workers are different from other people. How are they different?'
a) shorter than average b) pale and ugly c) thin-haired – even the women

1

CRAZY CURSES
1890

The idea of making mummies started with the strange story of Osiris. And it ends with the strange story of a mummy curse. Some people believe that if you disturb a mummy's grave you will meet a horrible hend ... I mean 'end'. The story is as true as the tale of Amen-Ra...

IN THE 1880s, FOUR EGYPTIAN ROBBERS DUG UP A MUMMY AND TOOK IT AWAY TO SELL...

I WILL GIVE YOU THREE YOUR SHARE OF THE MONEY AND I'LL KEEP THE MUMMY, I TAKE THE RISK THAT IT MAY BE WORTHLESS

SOUNDS FAIR ENOUGH

THE ROBBER TOOK IT TO HIS HOTEL ROOM. BUT ONE NIGHT HE SAID...

I AM GOING FOR A WALK!

HE WALKED INTO THE DESERT AND WAS NEVER SEEN AGAIN.

CURSE HIM! HEH! HEH!

THE SECOND ROBBER TOOK THE MUMMY HOME. BUT HE ARGUED WITH A SERVANT.

THAT MUMMY WILL BRING BAD LUCK!

THEN GET OUT. YOU ARE SACKED

THE SERVANT DREW A GUN AND SHOT THE ROBBER IN THE ARM.

BANG

AAAAGGGGH!

MUMMY!

THEY OPENED UP THE COFFIN AT THE MUSEUM AND EXAMINED THE MUMMY.

IN LIFE SHE WAS THE PRIESTESS, AMEN-RA, A WICKED WOMAN

SHE DIED IN 1500 BC

5

There are many such stories of curses. Old mummies bringing death and misery to the modern world. Are they true? Make up your own mind.

WHICH VILE VILLAIN ARE YOU?

Are you a gruesome ganster or a revolting revolutionary? Take the quiz and find out!

You're very angry with your friend. What do you do?

I just kill people for fun, mostly.

You seem to like killing people – but why?

If I kill people, my country will be a better place.

Mad, shouty, and fond of biting.

What's your proudest achievement?

What were you like when you were little?

As one of the vilest villains in history!

A real goody-goody – I always got the best marks.

How would you like to be remembered?

Some people will love me, others will hate me.

HE'S THE HEAD VILLAIN

What would you like for dinner?

Beat him to death with a baseball bat. Bada boom.

You're AL CAPONE

You love nice suits, money and being a gangster. You made loads of money out of smuggling, and killed anyone who got in your way. You got away with a life of crime for years, but in the end you went to prison for not paying taxes!

Invite him to a dinner party and make him wrestle with a lion. What fun!

You're EMPEROR ELAGABALUS

Wow – you're really, really mad – even for a Roman emperor (they're all a bit mad). You love making your friends eat live parrots and you think you're a Sun god. One day you tried to have your soldiers killed, but they decided to kill you instead … and you were murdered in a toilet!

HE'S OFF THE THRONE!

Overthrowing the king!

You're ROBESPIERRE

You're a brilliant leader, but you let power go to your head. You led the French Revolution and got rid of the king, but then you started killing anyone who disagreed with you. In the end, you got your head chopped off too.

Burning 280 people to death in just four years!

You're MARY TUDOR

You're clever, brave and stubborn, and you don't like people who disagree with you. You're a Catholic, and you had so many Protestants executed during your reign that you earned the nickname Bloody Mary.

Anything but chocolate – that's disgusting.

You're CHRISTOPHER COLUMBUS

You're adventurous and love to travel – but you can be selfish and cruel. When you discovered America in 1492, you kidnapped some of the people who lived there and took them back to Spain as slaves. In fact, you started the terrible slave trade that lasted another 400 years.

I'm not fussy – maybe some rotting meat and a couple of flies.

You're RATTUS RATTUS

You don't mean any harm, and you don't let anything go to waste –you'll even eat food off the floor. But your dirty habits can be dangerous. In the 1340s, you and your rat friends helped spread the Black Death which killed 75 million people.

GUILTY

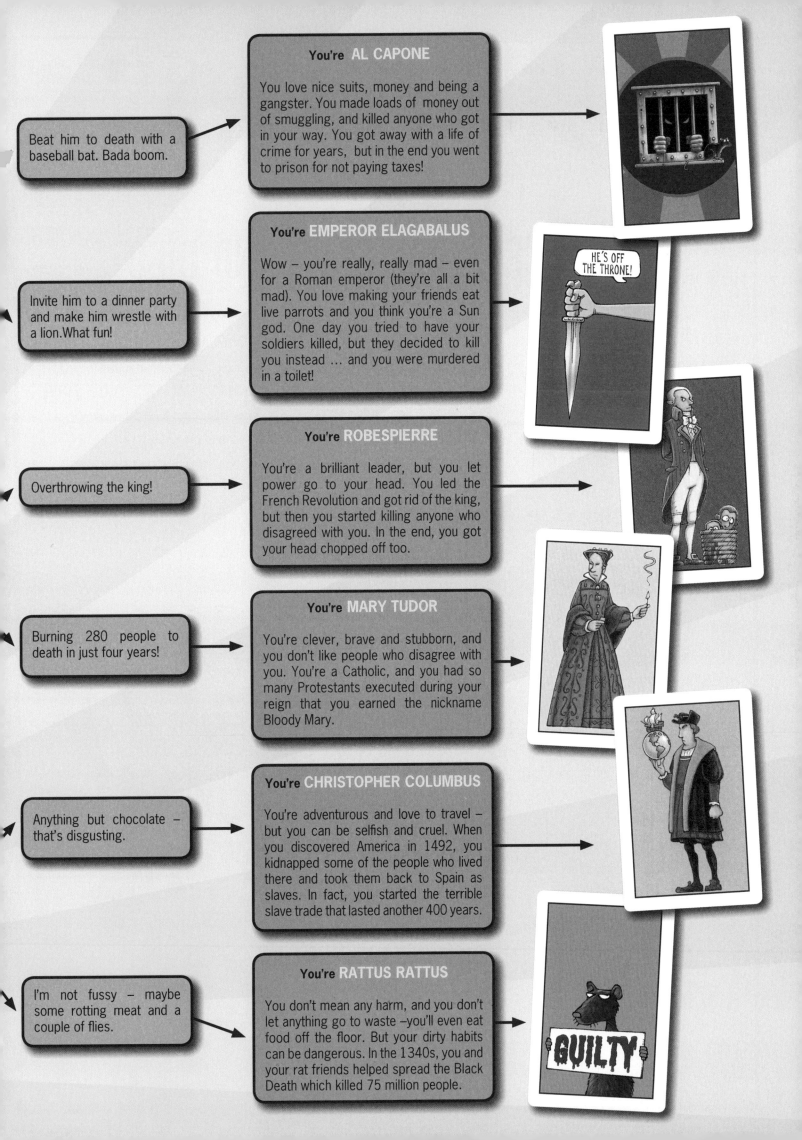

DIVORCED, BEHEADED AND DIED

Divorced, beheaded and died.
Divorced, beheaded, survived.
I'm Henry the Eighth, I had six sorry wives,
Some might say I ruined their lives.

I'm Henry the Eighth, I had six sorry wives,
Some might say I ruined their lives.
Catherine of Aragon was one,
She failed to give me a son.
I had to ask her for a divorce,
That broke her poor heart of course.
Young Anne Boleyn, she was two.
Had a daughter, the best she could do.
I said she fl irted with some other man,
And off for the chop went dear Anne.
Lovely Jane Seymour was three.
The love of a lifetime for me.
She gave me a son, little Prince Ed,
Then poor old Jane went and dropped dead.

Divorced, beheaded and died.
Divorced, beheaded, survived.
I'm Henry the Eighth, I had six sorry wives,
Some might say I ruined their lives.

Anne of Cleves came at four.
I fell for the portrait I saw.
Then laid eyes on her face and cried,
'She's a horse!
I must have another divorce.'
Catherine Howard was fi ve.
A child of nineteen, so alive.
She fl irted with others, no way to behave,
The axe sent young Cath to her grave.
Catherine Parr she was last,
By then all my best days were past.
I lay on my death-bed, aged just fi fty-fi ve,
Lucky Catherine the last stayed alive.
I mean how unfair!

Divorced, beheaded and died.
Divorced, beheaded, survived.
I'm Henry the Eighth, I had six sorry wives,
Some might say I ruined their lives.

Lyrics by Terry Deary

30

The Four Georges

GEORGE I

I took the throne of Eng-a-land,
Just cos I was Protestant,
A German prince whose English stank,
King George number One.

GEORGE II

I liked to argue – now, that's clear,
Especially with my father here.
Before I died of diarrhoea,
I fought with my son.

GEORGE III

I broke records with my 60-year reign.

GEORGE IV

And I broke the scales with my giant frame …

ALL

Born to rule over you (ooh, aah),
King George …

GEORGE IV
Four!
GEORGE III
Three!
GEORGE I
One!
GEORGE II
And Two!

ALL

You had to do what we told you to,
Just because our blood was blue.

GEORGE I

I was the hunk, girls adored me,
Ladies all swooned before me.
They would do anything for me,
Or I'd have their husbands killed.

GEORGE II

Had a war with Prince Charles, Bonnie.

GEORGE III

Everyone said I was funny.

GEORGE IV

I spent everyone's money.

ALL

Our subjects were not thrilled …

GEORGE I

I was the sad one!

GEORGE II

And I was the bad one!

GEORGE III

I was the mad one!

GEORGE IV

And I was the fat one!

ALL

(We were) Born to rule over you (ooh, aah), Georges …

GEORGE I
One!
GEORGE III
Three!
GEORGE IV
Four!
GEORGE II
And Two!

ALL

England's Kings …

GEORGES I & II

Though we were German too!

GEORGE IV

Him, then him,

GEORGE III

Then me, then you.

ALL

Born to rule over you (ooh, aah),

GEORGE II

Gorged on fruit, then I died on the loo.

GEORGE I

People hated us and we hated them too.

GEORGES III & IV

Born to rule over you.

GEORGES I & II

Born to rule over you (ooh, aah),

GEORGE III

I was as batty as a bonkers kangaroo.

GEORGE IV

And I would have been more at home in a zoo
And, now, our song, is through.

Lyrics by Dave Cohen (additional lyrics: Laurence Rickard and Caroline Norris)

CHARLES II RAP

CHARLES II

My name is, my name is, my name is – Charles the Second!

I love the people and the people love me,
So much that they restored the English monarchy.
I'm part Scottish-French-Italian, a little bit Dane,
But one hundred per cent party animal! – Champagne?

Spaniels I adored, named after me too,
Like me they were fun with a natty hair-do.
Is today my birthday? I can't recall,
Let's have a party anyway because I love a masked ball.

ALL

All hail the King
Of Bling, let's sing,
Bells ring, ding ding.

CHARLES II

I'm the King! Who brought back partying!

King Charles my daddy lost his throne and kings were banned.
They chopped off his head, then Olly Cromwell ruled the land.
Old Olly wasn't jolly, he was glum and he was proud,
Would be miserable as sin only 'sinning's not allowed'.

When Olly died the people said, 'Charlie me hearty,
Get rid of his dull laws, come back, we'd rather party.'
This action's what they called the Monarchy Restoration,
Which naturally was followed by a huge celebration.

ALL

The King, of Eng- (land say),
no sin to sing (okay!)
Or anything (all say).

CHARLES II

I'm the King! Who brought back partying!
Great London Fire was a whopper.
In my reign London city came a cropper,
So this King did what was right and proper,
Fought the fi re, proved I'm more than a bopper,
I'm a fi re-stopper!

Married Catherine Braganza, she was a love so true,
There would never be another, well maybe one or two:
Lucy Walter, Nell Gwynn, Moll Davis, Barbara Villiers,
You think that's bad but her name's not as silly as

Hortense Manzini.

As king I must admit I broke the wedding rules,
But who cares when I brought back the crown jewels?
I reinstated Christmas, make-up, sport and even plays,
I was the Merry Monarch, they were the Good Old Days.

ALL

When said, and done,
King Charles (that's me), did run,
Englun', for fun.

CHARLES II

I was the King! Loved by everyone. My song is done.

Party anyone?

Lyrics by Dave Cohen

PARTY ON!

JOKE MACHINE

Where was the Magna Carta signed?
At the bottom.

Why didn't chimney sweeps like going up chimneys?
It didn't soot them.

Why couldn't the pirates play cards?
The captain was standing on the deck.

Why did Stone Age people eat sloths?
Because fast food is bad for you.

What was the Middle Ages famous for?
Its knight life.

Why did the mammoth have a fur coat?
Because he'd have looked silly in an anorak.

What did the mummy say when his brains were pulled out of his nose?
'I'm losing my mind!'

Why did Christopher Columbus sail to America?
It was too far to swim.

What did one cannon say to the other?
'You're a blast!'

Why does it take pirates so long to learn the alphabet?
Because they spend years at c.

Why did Robin Hood only rob the rich?
Because the poor had nothing worth pinching.

How do you make a Victoria Cross?
Stand on her toes.

Where was Hadrian's Wall?
At the bottom of Hadrian's garden.

What do you call a Roman with a cold?
Julius Sneezer

What do you get in a five-star pyramid?
A tomb with a view.

Why did Henry VIII have so many wives?
He liked to chop and change.

What did Tutankhamun become on his tenth birthday?
A year older.

What's the capital of Greece?
G.

What do Alfred the Great and Winnie the Pooh have in common?
Their middle name.

What's purple and burns?
The Grape Fire of London.

What's the difference between a buffalo and a bison?
You can't wash your hands in a buffalo!

What's the definition of an archaeologist?
Someone whose career lies in ruins!

What happened when Elizabeth I burped?
She issued a royal pardon.

GRISLY GALLERY

How well do you know the heroes and villains of Horrible Histories?

oliver cromwell

1. I didn't like Christmas, or the royal family.
2. I did like chopping off heads.
3. I had my head stuck on a pole for 25 years.

Ⓐ *oliver Cromwell*

Richard the lionheart

1. I murdered my brother and nephews ... or so they say.
2. Shakespeare wrote a play about me.
3. Don't believe everything you've heard – I didn't have a hunchback!

Ⓐ *Richard the III*

1. I wanted the opening of Parliament to go off with a bang.
2. People think I was executed on a bonfire, but I was hanged, drawn and quartered.
3. People throw me a big party with fireworks every year on 5 November.

Ⓐ *Gui fawkes*

1. I was born in Stratford-upon-Avon.
2. I wrote lots of plays. One of them is about a prince whose name rhymes with 'omlette'.
3. I died on my birthday.

Ⓐ *Shakspear william*

1. My real name was Edward Teach.
2. I was captain of a ship named Queen Anne's Revenge.
3. I liked putting bits of rope under my hat and setting fire to them, to make me look scary.

Ⓐ *Black beard*

Well done!

1. I had bright red hair.
2. I really hated Romans.
3. Some say I'm buried under platform 8 of Kings Cross station in London.
a) Boudicea

1. I thought Russian tsars were a dis-tsar-ster.
2. I led the Red Terror, in which 280,000 people died.
3. I was bald, but I had a lovely goatie.
A) Lenin

1. I ruled longer than any other British monarch.
2. I was so sad when my husband died that I wore black clothes for the rest of my life.
3. Lots of things are named after me, including a delicious sponge cake and a place in Australia.
A Queen Victoria

1. I helped overthrow the king of France, but then I became emperor of France, which is pretty much the same thing.
2. I wanted to invade Britain, but I changed my mind when I met Lord Nelson.
A 3. I was defeated at the Battle of Waterloo.
Napolian bonaparte

1. I was king of Wessex.
2. I vanquished the Vikings.
3. I'm famous for burning some cakes ... but I didn't. I'm a great cook, me. I'm great at everything.
Alfred the Great

I NEVER FORGET A FACE!

ARMOUR DRAMA

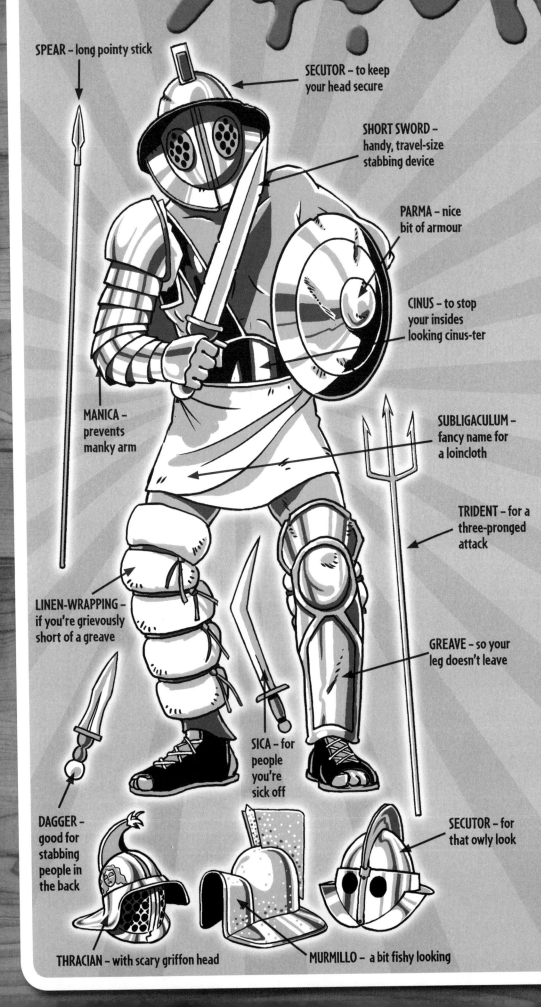

SPEAR – long pointy stick

SECUTOR – to keep your head secure

SHORT SWORD – handy, travel-size stabbing device

PARMA – nice bit of armour

CINUS – to stop your insides looking cinus-ter

MANICA – prevents manky arm

SUBLIGACULUM – fancy name for a loincloth

TRIDENT – for a three-pronged attack

LINEN-WRAPPING – if you're grievously short of a greave

GREAVE – so your leg doesn't leave

SICA – for people you're sick off

DAGGER – good for stabbing people in the back

THRACIAN – with scary griffon head

MURMILLO – a bit fishy looking

SECUTOR – for that owly look

Ding ding! It's a Horrible Histories face-off: in the blue corner we have a gruesome gladiator, and in the yellow corner there's a nasty knight. But who will win? Are the knight's weapons woeful? Or will the gladiator be 'armless?

GLADIATOR

Scare factor: 9

Shininess: 4

Speed: 10

Deadliness: 6

Strength: 10

Protection from armour: 4

Final score: 43

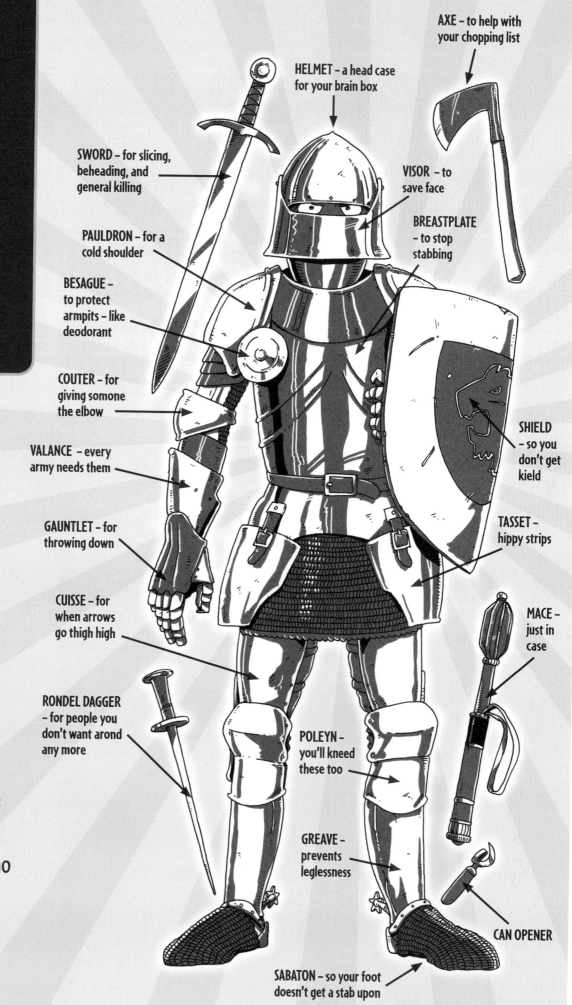

KNIGHT

Scare factor: 8
Shininess: 10
Speed: 4
Deadliness: 9
Strength: 8
Protection from armour: 10

Final score: 49

RESULT:

It was the knight's night!

It was close – the gladiator was strong and quick, but the knight's dagger made him stagger. In the end, his armour was no match for the axe.

SEE YOU LATER, GLADIATOR!

AXE – to help with your chopping list

HELMET – a head case for your brain box

SWORD – for slicing, beheading, and general killing

VISOR – to save face

BREASTPLATE – to stop stabbing

PAULDRON – for a cold shoulder

BESAGUE – to protect armpits – like deodorant

COUTER – for giving somone the elbow

SHIELD – so you don't get kield

VALANCE – every army needs them

TASSET – hippy strips

GAUNTLET – for throwing down

MACE – just in case

CUISSE – for when arrows go thigh high

RONDEL DAGGER – for people you don't want arond any more

POLEYN – you'll kneed these too

GREAVE – prevents leglessness

CAN OPENER

SABATON – so your foot doesn't get a stab upon

PUTRID PARTY GAMES

There ain't no party like a Horrible Histories party!
Put your friends in a horrible mood with these gory games.

HISTORICAL TRUTH OR DARE?

Roll a die, look at the number on the die and find the matching box, and choose – truth or dare?

1. TRUTH
What's the most horrible thing you've ever done to someone?

DARE
Choose someone and pretend to be their servant for the rest of the day. Call them 'My Lord' or 'My Lady'.

6. TRUTH
If you were the reincarnation of someone from history, who would it be?

DARE
Run around the room pretending your feet are on fire.

2. TRUTH
What's the most loathsome lie you've ever told?

DARE
Go outside and pour a glass of cold water over yourself, while singing your favourite Horrible Histories song. Don't stop singing till you get to the end!

5. TRUTH
If you had to be best friends with one of your teachers for the rest of your life, who would you choose?

DARE
Pretend you're dying of the plague, with sound effects, for three minutes.

4. TRUTH
Who would you choose to be locked in a castle dungeon with?

DARE
Behave like a rat until your next turn, and don't speak. (You can squeak if you like. But don't give anyone the Black Death.)

3. TRUTH
If you could spy on anyone in the world, who would you spy on?

DARE
You've just been awarded 'Horrible historian of the year'! Make an acceptance speech thanking everyone you know.

MUMMY MADNESS

Are your friends looking a little bit too ... alive? Then play Mummy Madness and help them get to the afterlife!

WHAT YOU NEED:

Two teams of fearless friends

Lots and lots of toilet paper – at least two rolls per team.

A putrid prize like a smelly sock (or a nice prize, if you insist)

HOW TO PLAY:

1. Each team chooses one person to be the mummy.

2. The other players wrap the mummy up in toilet paper until he or she is completely covered – except for the mouth, nose and eyes.

3. Make sure you wrap the legs separately so the mummy can walk around looking scary.

4. The first team to wrap their mummy up completely wins the putrid prize!

If this seems too easy, blindfold everyone in the team except the mummy!

AAARGH!

WHAT'S YOUR IDEAL JOB FROM HISTORY?

Are you a miserable miner or a secretive spy? Take the quiz and find out!

Is lying always wrong?

I want to do something I believe in!

Would you rather work with ordinary people or do something you really believe in?

I want to work with ordinary people, like me.

Yes – I know exactly what I want to do.

You meet a boy who has stolen something to buy medicine for his sick sister. What do you do?

Do you know what you want to be when you grow up?

No – it doesn't really matter as long as I can afford to eat.

Yes!

Are you afraid of the dark?

No.

THIS JOB IS THE PITS

Which animal are you most like?

No. I lie all the time! I like pretending I'm from Russia, and wearing disguises, too.

A SPY

You're brave, brilliant, and born to serve your country. You travel into enemy territory and pass secrets back to your government. You're an ace at cracking codes, a master of disguise, and you can speak lots of different languages. But can you hold up under torture? You'll have to if your true identity is discovered…

Yes. Liars should be locked alone in their rooms and fed bread and water.

A MONK OR NUN

You're more holy than your socks! You spend your life in the monastery (or nunnery) praying, working in the fields, helping the poor and needy, praying, sleeping in an unheated room, praying, eating foul mush, and writing books. (Tip for monks – want to know how to get the bald bit on the top of your head? Rub it with a stone.)

I tell him to bring his sister to my cottage, so I can cure her.

A WISE WOMAN

You're a very important person – people who can't afford to go to the doctor come to you instead. You cure people with herbs, and use the odd magic spell. But watch out – one minute people think you're a wise woman, and the next they're calling you a witch – and the next thing you know, you're being burned at the stake!

I report him to the authorities so he can be punished. Off with his head!

AN EXECUTIONER

You've got a good aim with an axe, a strong stomach, and you look good in black. You chop the heads off criminals (and people the king or queen just don't like very much). You don't have a very popular job, but don't worry, no one knows who you are – your name is kept secret, and you wear a hood so no one can recognize you.

A crow – I've got a head for heights.

A CHIMNEY SWEEP

Your job is perfect for children – you have to be tiny to fit up the chimneys. You work in hot, dark cramped conditions, cleaning away the soot from fireplaces, so it's too bad if you don't like small spaces or have asthma. Make sure you don't get stuck in the chimney or fall asleep on the job – your master will light a fire underneath you!

A mole – I like digging holes.

A MINER

Congratulations – you've got the dirtiest and most dangerous job of all! You work underground, digging up coal for 16 hours a day. If you think you're too young for a job like that, you're wrong – Victorian kids started working in the mines aged five. But watch out – a mining inspector said 'Mining gives more ways of dying than any other job.'

HIGH-SPEED HISTORY

WHICH KNIGHT IS WITCH?
FRANCE, 1428

BY 1430 IT WAS FOUL TO BE FRENCH. THE OLD KING CHARLES VI WAS MAD AND NOT FIT TO RULE. HIS SON, PRINCE CHARLES, WAS A BIT OF A WIMP AND NOT READY TO FIGHT THE ENGLISH INVADERS. MILLIONS OF FRENCH HAD BEEN KILLED OFF BY THE BLACK DEATH. IT ALL LOOKED PRETTY HOPELESS. THEN ALONG CAME A GIRL CALLED JOAN.

JOAN WAS A FARMER'S DAUGHTER. SHE LOOKED AFTER THE SHEEP IN THE FIELDS. A BORING JOB.

I SPY WITH MY LITTLE EYE, SOMETHING BEGINNING WITH 'S'

WHAT'S SHE DOING?

PLAYING SHEPHERD'S SPY ... SHEPHERD'S PIE ... GEDDIT?

IT WAS A LONELY JOB. THERE WAS NO ONE TO TALK TO.

I LOVE EWE

SHE SHOULD SEE A DOC

OR A FLOCK

BUT SOON A MESSENGER ARRIVED WITH SHOCKING NEWS...

MY LORD ... PRINCE CHARLES HAS JUST SUFFERED A TERRIBLE DEFEAT AT ORLÉANS!

AMAZING! MAYBE THIS JOAN OF ARC IS NOT SO MAD AFTER ALL. I WILL SEND A TROOP OF SOLDIERS TO TAKE YOU TO THE PRINCE

PRINCE CHARLES OF FRANCE, AND HIS MUM, MET JOAN...

SHE MUST BE MAD, MOTHER

MAYBE. BUT YOU HAVE NOTHING TO LOSE. THE ENGLISH AND THEIR FRIENDS IN BURGUNDY ARE BEATING US TIME AFTER TIME

THE ANGELS SAID YOU WOULD

JOAN WAS HIT BY A STONE CANNONBALL ON THE HELMET, BUT SURVIVED...

STONE OF ARC

JOAN'S ARMY CAPTURED THE CITY OF REIMS SO PRINCE CHARLES COULD BE CROWNED KING OF FRANCE IN THE CATHEDRAL.

BUT THE WAR GOES ON UNTIL WE HAVE DRIVEN THE ENGLISH OUT OF FRANCE

OH, I SUPPOSE SO. I'M NOT THAT BOTHERED NOW I'M KING

BUT IN 1430 JOAN WAS CAPTURED BY BURGUNDY SOLDIERS ON THE BATTLEFIELD. AS YOU KNOW, KNIGHTS WERE SOLD TO THEIR FAMILY FOR A RANSOM. BUT JOAN'S FAMILY WERE POOR...

HOW MUCH? WE'D HAVE TO SELL THE FARM AND ALL OUR SHEEP FOR SLAUGHTER FOR A DAUGHTER

WE'D BE RUINED

AND WE'D BE PRETTY RUINED TOO

Joan died a cruel death. Her charred body was burned three times till there was nothing but ash. The ash was scattered on the river. But killing her didn't help the English much. Joan the knight had broken the English power and they never got it back. In the end Prince Charles drove them out to end the Hundred Years War. The knights needed to find new wars to fight.

4

COUGH COUGH

SPOT THE LOT - 8 DIFFERENCES TO FIND

TALK LIKE A PIRATE

Thinking of running away to sea on Blackbeard's boat?
If you don't want to be spotted as a lousy landlubber, learn to talk like a pirate.
Here are a few words to get you started...

Ahoy 'Ahoy' means 'hello'. Most pirates aren't polite enough to use this word.

Avast ye If you see a ship you want to capture you have to tell it to stop. Do NOT shout, 'Excuse me, but would you mind slowing down so I can rob you?' Shout 'Avast ye!' It means 'Stop ... or else!'

Aye 'Yes'. You should say this to almost everything your captain asks you. Unless he asks, 'Did you steal the last of my biscuits, you bilge rat?'

Aye aye 'I'll do that right away, captain.'

Bilge The very bottom of the ship. This is where water seeps in, rats live and all the filth of the ship ends up. It stinks and the air down there is deadly. Never call a pirate a bilge rat or he may take a cutlass to your cheeky tongue.

Hairy Willy Dried fish. It might look disgusting, but it's better than nothing ... just remember you're eating something pirates call 'Hairy Willy'.

Heave to Want a ship to stop? then call out 'heave to' – that means 'stand still. It has nothing to do with 'heaving overboard' which is what you'd do if you found an enemy on your ship.

Landlubber A 'lubber' is a clumsy person on a ship, who'd be happier on land. If you really want a cutlass up your nose, call a pirate a 'landlubber'.

Scurvy knave Scurvy means mean, despicable and generally rotten or scabby. And a 'knave' is a villain. So scurvy knave or scabby villain: take your pick – or pick your scab.

Scuttle If you're in danger from attack by another ship, you may want to sink your own ship and row off in a lifeboat. Do NOT say, 'Poke a little hole in the boat and let it sink.' To sink your own ship is to 'scuttle' it.

Shiver me timbers If a ship gets a sudden blast from a cannon then its masts ('timbers') are shaken (or 'shivered'). So a shocked ship has shivered timbers. If YOU get a shock then don't say, 'Goodness me, I am surprised!', say 'Shiver me timbers!'

Slops Slops were the 1700s sailor word for trousers. Sailors were among the first people to wear them.

Swabbie A swab was a mop made of rope ends or threads. A swabbie had the job of mopping the deck – cleaning up the blood and guts after a fight.

CRAZY CURES

CURES FOR TOOTHACHE

STONE AGE Eat hollyhock flowers.

SAXON Boil a holly leaf, lay it on a saucer of water, raise to your mouth and yawn.

STUART Scratch the gum with a new nail and then drive the nail into a tree.

GEORGIAN Burn the ear with hot poker.

CURES FOR SNAKE BITES

ROMAN Grind up fennel with wine and pour it in the nostrils, while rubbing pig droppings on the wound.

SAXON Get some wood from a tree grown in heaven and press it to the wound.

GEORGIAN Kill a chicken, rip out its guts and place them on the wound while still warm.

CURES FOR DIARRHOEA

ANCIENT EGYPTIAN Eat gruel, green onions, honey, wax and water. Yum.

INCA Chew coca leaves.

CURES FOR A HEADACHE

STONE AGE AND ROMAN Drill a hole in the skull.

SAXON Find some swallow-chicks, cut their stomachs open and look for some little stones. Tie the stones up in a small bag and put it on your head.

MIDDLE AGES Take off your hat so the harmful fumes can escape from your head.

INCA Gouge a hole between the eyes with glass knife.

TUDOR Press a hangman's rope to the neck.

CURES FOR EYE PROBLEMS

ANCIENT EGYPTIAN Poor eyesight at night: eat roasted, crushed ox liver.

Cataracts: eat tortoise brain and honey.

Blindness: Mash a pig's eye with red ochre and pour it into the ear.

SAXON Swollen eyelid: cut it out with a knife.

GEORGIAN Stye: rub it with the tail of a black cat.

CURES FOR BALDNESS

SAXON Burn bees and rub the ash on your head.

TUDOR Smear your head with fox grease, garlic and vinegar.

CURES FOR THE PLAGUE

MIDDLE AGES
- Wear a magpie's beak around your neck.
- Sit in a sewer.
- Drink ten-year-old treacle.
- Swallow crushed emeralds.
- Eat arsenic (a poison).
- Shave a live chicken's bottom and strap it to the plaguey sores.
- Move from town to town flogging yourself with a whip.

TUDOR Place a freshly killed pigeon on the sores.

CURES FOR A COLD

MIDDLE AGES Put mustard and onions up your nose.

VICTORIAN Wrap a sweaty sock around your neck.

CURES FOR FEVER

INCA (for a baby) Wash the baby in a bowl of its family's pee, and give it some to drink.

STUART Cut a pigeon in half and place one half on each foot.

CURES FOR GOUT (SWOLLEN JOINTS)

MIDDLE AGES Use a plaster made of goat droppings, rosemary and honey.

TUDOR Boil a red-haired dog in oil, add worms, pig marrow and herbs. Place the mixture on the affected area.

CURES FOR BRUISES

ROMAN Treat with unwashed sheep's wool, dipped in animal fat.

MIDDLE AGES Make a plaster out of bacon fat and flour.

CURE MOST LIKELY TO GET YOU LOCKED UP

Ambrose Pare, of France, was called a 'great' surgeon because he learned how to treat soldiers wounded in battle. But one of his ointments for a wound was just a little sick:

YOU NEED:
Two new-born puppies, 1/2 kg earthworms, 1 kg lily oil, 1/2 kg turpentine, 25 g of brandy.

TO MAKE:
Heat the oil and boil the puppies alive. Drown the earthworms in white wine, and add them. Boil and strain. Add the brandy and turpentine. Mix well. Rub the mixture into the wound.

BARMY BRITAIN

Think Britain is great? Think again! Here are some of the maddest and baddest things that have ever happened in Britain.

An Irish explorer in Africa bought an eleven-year-old girl and sold her to cannibals, so he could watch how they killed, cooked and ate her.

A Brit Chief of Police in Africa used human skulls to decorate his flower beds.

Henry VIII had 72,000 people executed, including two of his wives and lots of his friends.

Henry VIII didn't kill his first wife, Catherine of Aragon but he was so pleased when she died that he held a thanksgiving church service followed by a huge party!

In bad old Britain you could be hanged for wearing a disguise! Fancy dress parties would have turned into fancy death parties.

Other crimes you could be hanged for: stealing anything worth more than five shillings (25p), or being in the company of gypsies.

Starving Saxons didn't bury their dead friends – they ate them.

Starving Saxons ate dogs, cats and rats, too.

The ancient Scottish Attacotti tribe hunted humans and ate their brains. Nice!

George III was truly mad. He once tried to adopt a pillow as a son, and had a chat with a tree because he thought it was the King of Prussia.

George III also believed he was dead for a while, and wore black mourning clothes out of respect.

After Charles I had his head chopped off it was sewn back on to his body so his family could pay their last respects.

Years after Charles I was buried, a lousy lord stole his neck bone from his tomb and used it to serve salt to his dinner guests!

There used to be a royal zoo at the Tower of London, with lions, tigers and an elephant.

The Tower of London was used as a prison for German spies during the First World War. Eleven spies were shot dead there.

Cruel Oliver Cromwell ruled Britain after Charles I's executuon. He was a Puritan (very religious) and hated fun, so he cancelled Christmas and had theatres pulled down.

Puritan children were given names like 'Sorry-for-sin', 'Helpless' and 'Silence'.

In the 1800s the average Brit workman worked 96 hours a week for 40p. He survived on bread and butter, except on Sundays when he ate half a bullocks head.

Wales was the last country to press a man to death. To press a man to death you piled stones on top of him till he was squashed like a hedgehog under a cartwheel.

In 1888, a serial killer named Jack the Ripper killed five (maybe more) women in London. He cut out their internal organs and laid them around the bodies. He was never caught. (Don't worry though – he's either 150ish or dead. Either way, you're safe.)

During the Second World War, people in London sheltered from bombs in Underground stations. Some people slept in Tube stations, and had to go to the toilet in a bucket!

IT'S ALL TRUE!

1 Henry V took the throne in 1413 and married Catherine. Two hundred and thirty years later the writer Samuel Pepys kissed her. How? (Clue: everyone likes a kiss from their mummy)

Answer: Catherine's corpse was turned into a mummy and put on show next to the coffin of Henry V. People could look at her for a couple of pennies and she stayed there for almost 300 years. Samuel Pepys kissed the mummy – weird!

2 Historians argue about exactly who King Arthur was. One thing's for certain. Arthur was not his proper name – just a nickname. What does 'Arthur' mean?
a) He who fights on two sides.
b) Great leader of 100 battles.
c) Bear.

Answer: c)

3 Some of the stones used to make Stonehenge were carried from a site in Wales nearly 400 km away. True or false?

TRUE. Don't envy the builders on that job!

4 There was no Saxon soap power. What did they make their own detergent from?
a) Snot.
b) Pee.
c) Spit.

Answer: b)

5 What was a 'bung-napper' in Stuart times?
a) A sleepwalker.
b) A purse-snatcher.
c) A dustman.

Answer: b)

6 Some Norman women used the poisonous deadly nightshade plant to make their eyes more attractive. True or false?

TRUE. But very rarely! Norman women in Western Europe used hardly any make-up. Rich women in Eastern Europe used lip colour and drops of deadly nightshade to make the black centre of the eyes (the pupils) open wide. Gorgeous.

7 The Normans enjoyed Easter eggs. True or false?

TRUE. During Lent (the weeks before Easter) the Church did not allow Christians to eat eggs. So housewives would save up all their eggs to have as a special treat on Easter Day. They would be boiled and coloured with natural dye – try boiling an egg with onion skins and see what happens! Have your boiled eggs blessed by a priest and scoff them.

8 In the First World War, British dogs were horses. True or false.

TRUE. The British Army supplied all the animals they needed, but to keep everything simple they called all the animals 'horses'.

9 What did the Celts put on their ponies to protect them during races?
a) Shin guards (like footballers wear) made of whale bones.
b) Crash-helmets made of metal.
c) Leather boots cushioned with sheepskin.

Answer: b) Pony caps, with holes for the ears, have been found at Celtic sites in the Shetlands.

10 Elizabeth I's godson, Sir John Harrington, disgraced himself by making rude remarks to her ladies-in-waiting. She banished him. He went off and invented something that was so useful she forgave him. What? (Clue: flushed with success?)

A flushing toilet. It took him six years to invent it but Liz loved his loo.

11 In 1940, a man was arrested for lighting a cigarette. Why?
a) He was breaking the blackout laws.
b) Smoking was illegal in Britain until 1949.
c) He was giving a secret sign to a German spy nearby.

Answer: a)

12 In 1653, Charles Culpepper wrote about a plant that clears bad chests, cures headaches, worms and indigestion, and cleared lice. What was this wonder plant?
a) Tobacco.
b) Deadly nightshade.
c) Larkspur.

Answer: a)

GOOD LUCK!

13 Which scary Saxon brothers did Vortigern ask to help him beat the Picts?
a) Hengest and Horsa
b) Gildas and Greybeard
c) Ambrosius and Arthur

Answer: a)

14 Which of the following new food fads became popular in Stuart Britain?
a) Eating sandwiches.
b) Eating with knives.
c) Drinking tea.

Answer: c)

15 Why did many Georgian pirates wear gold earrings?
a) It was a sign of their status and success.
b) They believed it helped them see better.
c) They thought it made them look scarier.

Answer: b)

16 What did sailors in Nelson's navy do with the horribly hard cheese they were given to eat?
a) They used it in mouse traps – the ice broken their teeth and the starved to death.
b) They carved the cheese with their knives to make buttons for their coats.
c) They used the cheese to play games like shove ha'penny on the deck.

Answer: b)

17 How was Lord Nelson's body brought home after his death at Trafalgar in 1805? (Clue: not a barrel of laughs)

Answer: Pickled in a barrel of brandy. It preserved the body – and the sailors drank the brandy afterwards!

18 What was the punishment for leaving fingermarks and ink blots on your schoolwork in Victorian times?
a) Being caned (so your hands were sore and you'd probably make even more mess).
b) Having to do the work all over again.
c) Death.

Answer: a)

19 Victoria was the shortest monarch ever to sit on the British throne (she needed a stepladder to reach it). True or false?

TRUE. Victoria wasn't even five feet tall (she probably didn't use a stepladder to reach the throne, though).

20 Joseph Merrick was cruelly put on show to the ghoulish Victorian public because of an unusual illness. What was Merrick's nickname?
a) The Giraffe Man
b) The Gorilla Man
c) The Elephant Man

Answer: c)

21 During the First World War the women who worked with TNT explosive were nicknamed 'canaries'. Why?
a) They were so happy they sang like canaries while they worked.
b) The TNT caused their hair to turn canary yellow.
c) Because the factory owners were getting 'cheep' labour.

Answer: b)

22 In 1376 Edward III died and ten-year-old Richard II was crowned the following year. He walked into Westminster but was carried out. Why? (Clue: zzzzz)

Answer: Richard collapsed under the strain of the excitement – and the heavy robes and crown.

23 Henry VII's no. 2, Anne Boleyn, needed the toilet a lot during her coronation. Her ladies-in-waiting kept her potty handy...?
a) Under the table.
b) In a room close by.
c) On the throne.

Answer: a)

24 King Edward I of England once set up a tournament to give his knights a bit of practice, but he made the knights agree to use a sword made out of what?
a) Rubber.
b) Blunt steel.
c) Whalebone

Answer: c) Edward's 38 knights in the 1278 tournament had whalebone swords, 'armour' made from boiled leather – hard but light – and wooden shields. Clever Ed. He remembered his first tournament 20 years before where two knights were killed and another brain-damaged. He saved the sharp steel and hot blood for the battlefields of Scotland and Wales.

25 Knight errant Ulrich von Liechtenstein received a message from lady who was surprised to see that he had a particular finger. She thought he had lost the finger fighting in a tournament for her. What did he do?
a) Cut off a peasant's finger and sent it to the lady.
b) Cut off his own finger and sent it to her.
c) Had a model of the finger made from solid gold and sent to her.

Answer: b) Ulrich was as nutty a knight as you could ever wish to meet. He is said to have cut off his finger for the honour of the lady. It's just as well the lady didn't hear he'd lost his head!

26 During the Second World War, how would you know if the Germans had dropped mustard gas in your city? (Clue: it might be on a post-it note)

Answer: Look at the top of a post-box. They were painted yellow or green, which would stain if mustard gas got on it.

27 England was created when the Angles and the Saxons took over the south-east of Britain in ad 520. What did they call their new land?
a) Angle-land
b) Saxonia
c) Engal-land

Answer: a) They called it Angle-land, which eventually became England.

28 You know all about Halloween, of course, but what would you do on 31 October if you were a Celt? (Clue: It's not a trick question)

Answer: You'd dress in a scary costume to ward off the spirits. No trick or treating, though.

29 In 1747 Lord Lovat became the last person to be beheaded in the Tower of London. As he went to his death 20 other innocent people died. How? (Clue: curiosity killed the cat)

Answer: Spectators crowded on to wooden stands to watch Lovat get lopped. The stands collapsed and killed 20 people. Served them right.

30 Why did Queen Anne's doctors shave her head and cover her feet in garlic? (Clue: sick idea)

Answer: They were trying to cure her illness. They also blistered her skin with hot irons and gave her medicines to make her vomit. She died – and was probably glad to go.

31 What did the Saxons do if their dinner fell on the floor amongst the dog-droppings?
a) They wiped it off and ate it.
b) They gave it to the dog.
c) The children had it for tea the following day.

Answer: a) They'd wipe it off and make a sign of the cross to ward of evil spirits, before eating it. Makes school dinners seem tasty, doesn't it?

32 In 1545 Henry VIII went to watch his magnificent warship, the *Mary Rose*, set sail to sort out the French. What did *Mary Rose* do to surprise the king? (Clue: behaves in a fishy manner)

Answer: Rolled over and sank. It may have been top heavy with guns and men and the boat was upset. Henry was upset too – but 500 people on board were dead upset. Simply dead, in fact.

33 Copy-cat Blackpool built a copy of the Eiffel Tower in 1894. But is the Blackpool Tower bigger or smaller than the French one?

Answer: Smaller. Blackpool Tower is only half the height of the Eiffel Tower – but people falling off the top end up with exactly the same amount of deadness.

34 Sir Robert Peel created the police force, but the bobbies couldn't stop him dying in a traffic accident. How did he die?
a) He was crushed under the wheels of a carriage while crossing the road. Splat!!!
b) He was crossing a railway line when a train hit his coach. Splinter!!!
c) He fell off his horse and the horse fell on top of him. Scrunch!!!

Answer: c) In July 1850 Bob Peel was riding up Constitution Hill in London when he fell and his horse fell on top of him. This was not good for his health. Do not try it at home – or on Constitution Hill.

35 In the 1600s children in southwest England were forbidden to smoke. True or false?

False. Children in Somerset, Devon and Cornwall actually took their clay pipes to school. Smoking was considered healthy then. Pupils at Eton were ordered to smoke during the plague years because it was said to help you avoid the disease. The smell could well have sent the plague-rats packing.

36 What souvenir could you buy at the coronation of Charles II?
a) A slice of coronation cake.
b) A coronation mug.
c) A piece of Charles's coronation robe.

Answer: b) They were the first coronation souvenirs sold in Britain.

37 If you lived in Britain in 1916 and wanted to know what it was like in the trenches, you could visit some. Where?
a) On the French side of the Western Front near the town of Ypres.
b) Behind the German lines, near Berlin.
c) In Blackpool.

Answer: c) That's right, Blackpool. Soldiers recovering from wounds built replicas of the trenches at Loos. (That was a battlefield on the Western Front, not a toilet.) German people could visit the same sort of thing in Berlin.

38 In 1502, the first European to taste chocolate hated it. Who was it?
a) Christopher Columbus.
b) Henry VIII (when he was an 11-year-old prince).
c) Henry VII's pet dog who pinched it from the palace kitchen and was sick.

Answer: a) Columbus had discovered America in 1492. Ten years later he was visiting the Gulf of Honduras when natives offered him a drink of xocoatl (pronounced chocoatl). It was mixed with honey and spices and served cold and frosty. Columbus drank it politely but said, 'Yeuch!' Still, he brought some beans back to Europe and now it's a billion-pound industry.

39 In 1500 the first cookery book was published in the English language. What was it called?
a) The Two Fat Lardies
b) Filling Feasts for 1500
c) The Boke of Cokery

Answer: c) 'Cokery' was just the Tudor way of writing cookery – it had nothing to do with drinking Coke ... or eating lumps of coke for that matter.

40 Some Elizabethans believed that going to the theatre was the cause of the plague. True or false?

TRUE. In the 1590s the plague spread though Tudor England repeatedly – usually in the summer. London magistrates closed the theatre to stop it spreading. But some religious people believed the theatre caused the plague. They said the theatre was wicked and God punished theatre-goers by giving them the plague.

41 The Normans ate canaries on toast. True or false?

False. The Normans brought canaries from the Canary Islands (believe it or not). The Canary Islanders loved to eat the little feathered foodstuff but the Normans wanted them for their singing.

42 A Norman knight swore to prove his love for a lady. She told him to go off and pick up all the stones on the beaches of Brittany. What did he do?
a) Collected an army to do the job and won the heart of the lady.
b) Tried to do it himself but hurt his back and never fought again.
c) Sulked and went to bed for two years.

Answer: c) The knight had asked for it really. Never ask a lady, 'What can I do to win your love?' She may not want her love to be won and might set an impossible task!

PENS DOWN

AWESOME ANSWERS

Horrible Hotseat p8-9

1. **True!** Tooth drills made of flint have been found in Pakistan that date from 9,000 years ago!

2. **False!** They could only be rung to warn that the Germans had invaded.

3. **False!** They fought naked! They probably thought it would scare their enemies. Seems like a daft idea with all those swords flying around. Not to mention chilly.

4. **True!** France ordered every taxi cab in Paris to be available to take soldiers to the front line so they'd get there in time for the big battle.

5. **False!** They actually hated him and his stories. In fact, they hated him so much that they threw him off a cliff.

6. **False!** They threw sawdust over her!

7. **True!** It probably didn't work, but at least it gave the patient something to suck on...

8. **False!** Only the Incan Emperor was allowed to marry his sister. It was meant to keep his royal blood pure.

9. **True!** He invented 1,700 new words, including 'hurry', 'accomodation' and 'generous'!

10. **False!** She was famous for having rotten teeth, but they didn't kill her. She caught a cold and never recovered.

Lonely Hearts x2 p12

Henry VIII

Elizabeth I

Dear Ratty x2 p13

George VI

Pachacuti

Egypt spot the lot p16-17

Did you spot all 11?

Would you rather? p18

...live in a house made out of pig poo (Savage Saxons) or sleep in a Tube station every night (Londoners during the Second World War)?

...pee in your boots to soften them up (First World War soldiers) or wash your clothes with wee (Measly Middle Ages)?

...wear lipstick made of crushed beetles or white make-up made of poisonous lead (both Tudor women)?

...work as a 'dredger-man', pulling dead bodies out of the river, or spend all day cleaning chimneys and risk being burned to death (Victorians)?

...eat barbecued cows' lungs (Stone Age) or roast guineapig (Incas)?

...wear a skirt so wide you can't walk through doors, (Georgians) or an iron corset so tight you keep fainting (Tudors)?

Wordsearch p19

Slum Street p22-23

1c), 2b), 3a), 4b), 5a), 6c), 7b), 8c), 9c), 10a), 11c), 12c), 13c), 14b), 15a), 16b), 17a), 18a), 19a b & c), 20c).

Grisly Gallery p36-37

Oliver Cromwell

Richard the Lionheart

Boudica

Lenin

Queen Victoria

Guy Fawkes

William Shakespeare

Blackbeard

Napoleon

Alfred the Great

Where's Ratty (Tudor street) p38-39

Did you find all 10?

Spot the lot p50

Did you spot all 8?